D0427210

DISCARD

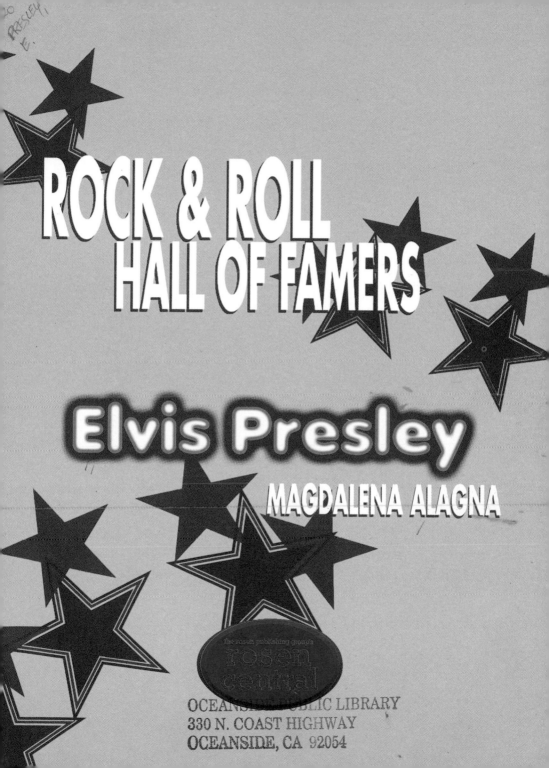

ROCK & ROLL
HALL OF FAMERS

Elvis Presley

MAGDALENA ALAGNA

the rosen publishing group's
rosen
central

Published in 2002 by The Rosen Publishing Group, Inc.
29 East 21st Street, New York, NY 10010

Copyright © 2002 by The Rosen Publishing Group, Inc.

First Edition

Library of Congress Cataloging-in-Publication Data

Alagna, Magdalena.
Elvis Presley / by Magdalena Alagna.– 1st ed.
p. cm. — (Rock & roll hall of famers)
Includes discography, filmography, list of Web sites,
bibliographical references, and index.
ISBN 0-8239-3524-8 (library binding)
1. Presley, Elvis, 1935–1977—Juvenile literature. 2. Rock musicians—
United States—Biography—Juvenile literature. [1. Presley, Elvis,
1935–1977. 2. Singers. 3. Rock music.] I. Title. II. Series.
ML3930.P73 A43 2002
782.42166'092—dc21   4136

                                      2001003888

Manufactured in the United States of America

CONTENTS

Elvis Presley, "the King of Rock and Roll," is still one of the most popular musicians of all time.

Introduction

Elvis Presley burst
onto the music
scene in the
mid-1950s and
served as the
catalyst for
rock and roll.
Elvis had more
number-one records
and starring movie roles
than any other rock
and roll performer.
He had 126 gold and
platinum records and
114 songs on the Top
40 charts. He starred
in thirty-three movies.
His songs were on the

charts every year from 1956 until 1977, the year
he died. John Lennon of the Beatles once
declared, "Before Elvis, there was nothing."

The phrase "rock and roll" is generally
attributed to Cleveland DJ Alan Freed. Freed was
one of the few white radio personalities, along
with the charismatic Dewey Phillips in Memphis,
Tennessee, to play black R & B, or rhythm and
blues, music in the early 1950s. Elvis may not have
created rock and roll, but he was dubbed its king,
and there has never been another performer to
challenge his claim to the title. He was part of a
new wave of rock and roll artists that included
Carl Perkins (who, along with Elvis, started out on
Sun Records), Johnny Cash, Buddy Holly, Roy
Orbison, and Jerry Lee Lewis. Elvis Presley was the
first artist to personify rock and roll.

Elvis, in his person as well as his music, was a
rock revolutionary. With his suggestive dance
moves that shocked and delighted audiences,
"Elvis the Pelvis," who earned his nickname for
the sexy dance moves he did onstage, was
blamed for single-handedly releasing the pent-up
sexual frustrations of 1950s youth. Also, he

Elvis Presley, with his singing and suggestive dance moves onstage, drove audiences wild.

helped to break down racial barriers by popularizing R & B and gospel music. Elvis always publicly acknowledged his debt to black R & B and gospel musicians.

Elvis was at the forefront of the musical revolution that gave voice to a generation and redefined music forever. Artists as widely diverse as John Lennon, Bob Dylan, Gene

Vincent, Paul McCartney, Billy Joel, and Nick Cave were influenced by Elvis Presley. It is doubtful whether one can find a rock musician who does not acknowledge his or her debt to Elvis Presley.

The story of Elvis Presley's success has as much to do with his manager, "Colonel" Tom Parker, as it does with the artist himself. Tom Parker bought Elvis's contract from Sun Records, and he helped to make the "Hillbilly Cat" into a rock and roll legend whose fame would grow to a cult bordering on the religious, even decades after his death. Thousands of fans flock every year to Graceland, Elvis's flamboyant mansion in Memphis. It is one of the most visited residences in the United States, second only to the White House.

Part of Elvis's popularity in the 1950s came from the fact that he was perfectly poised for musical stardom. He happened on the music scene in Memphis, Tennessee, one of the hottest places in the country then for R & B, at a time when America was eager for a raw, new sound. Elvis Presley's success also was due in large part

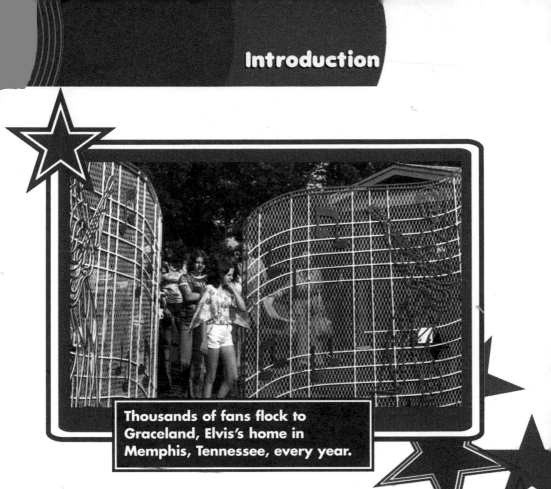

Thousands of fans flock to Graceland, Elvis's home in Memphis, Tennessee, every year.

to the calculated formation of his persona and the marketing, promotion, and merchandising of that persona in movies and memorabilia, which strikes us today as the precursor to the hyping of boy bands such as 'N Sync. Elvis merchandise included everything from wristwatches to socks to neck scarves bearing Elvis's image!

It can be said that the 1950s were Elvis's recording years, the 1960s were his movie years, and the 1970s were his Las Vegas years. His long and glorious career survived a two-year absence from the eyes of his adoring public, when he was serving in the army. He appeared on television to sing with Frank Sinatra, one of the most famous crooners of the 1940s, invited the Beatles to Graceland for a game of pool, and appeared in the world's first concert broadcast worldwide via satellite. He married Priscilla Beaulieu after dating some of the steamiest starlets of his day, such as his *Viva Las Vegas* costar Ann-Margret. His divorce from Priscilla in 1973 appeared to strike him a blow from which he never recovered.

The phenomenon of Elvis's career plateau throughout the sixties, his comeback in 1968, and the tabloid tragedy of his death in 1977 seem almost separate stories from the tale of his rise to music superstardom in the 1950s. Who was Elvis Presley, the man and the musician, and why do we continue to worship him as the king of rock and roll?

1

Elvis's Childhood

Elvis was born and raised in East Tupelo, Mississippi. It was a poor neighborhood in a poor farming community. Elvis's mother, born Gladys Love Smith, had met Vernon Elvis Presley at the First Assembly of God Church in East Tupelo. Vernon Elvis Presley was not even seventeen years old when he met Gladys, but Vernon and Gladys eloped and were married

Elvis, flanked by his father, Vernon Elvis Presley, and his mother, Gladys Presley

less than eight weeks after they met. Vernon lied on the marriage certificate, saying he was twenty-two, and Gladys took two years off her age, saying she was nineteen, although she was twenty-one at the time (four years older than Vernon).

After one year of marriage, Vernon and Gladys welcomed a son into the family. Elvis was

Understanding the Political Climate

Blacks and whites had fought side by side during World War II, unlike during peacetime, when much of America was segregated. Segregation meant that blacks and whites were separated as much as possible. There were different rest rooms for blacks and whites in many public buildings. Many businesses, such as theaters, had blacks-only or whites-only nights. There were even different schools for blacks and for whites. Segregation ensured that people of different races lived in two separate worlds, but this started to change slowly after WWII. Popular music at the time was evidence of the changing political climate. Elvis, by popularizing R & B, broke down racial barriers and introduced the world to "race" music, which is what R & B was called before 1949.

born on January 8, 1935. He was born in the two-room shack that Vernon had built with his brother Vester. It was a difficult labor; Gladys was carrying twins. The first twin, named Jessie Garon, was stillborn, meaning he was born dead. The second twin, born thirty-five minutes later, was named Elvis Aron. Elvis visited Jessie's grave often as a child, and he frequently mentioned his brother throughout his life.

Early Musical Influences: Hillbilly, Gospel, and the Blues

Radio was the Presleys' main form of entertainment. Elvis grew up listening to bluegrass, country and western (called hillbilly), R & B, gospel, and popular music, which, at the time, was big-band music. Later, crooning ballads by singers like Dean Martin and Frank Sinatra were Elvis's favorite kind of music.

Elvis sang both at home and at church with his parents. He was fascinated with church music. The First Assembly of God Church featured beautiful gospel quartets, or groups of four singers. Elvis would love gospel music all of his life. He especially loved the Statesmen and admired Statesman Jake Hess's vocal technique, but he also liked the Blackwood Brothers. These were two popular gospel quartets that influenced Elvis. It is apparent in some of his later gospel work on the album *How Great Thou Art* that Jake Hess particularly influenced Elvis's vocal style.

Elvis listened to the radio station WELO, which sponsored the *Black and White Jamboree.* Mississippi Slim, one of Elvis's musical influences, worked at WELO. He hosted a program called *Singin' and Pickin'*

Fun Fact!

In 1944, when he was ten, Elvis Presley stood on a chair and, unaccompanied, sang at the Mississippi-Alabama Fair and Dairy Show, at the fairgrounds in downtown Tupelo. He sang "Old Shep," a song about a boy and his dog.

15

Hillbilly, which was on before the *Jamboree.* Elvis went to the radio station almost every Saturday afternoon to see the *Jamboree.*

The Birthday Present

Elvis got his first guitar as a present for his eleventh birthday. Some accounts say that he wanted a bicycle instead; others say a rifle. Elvis's uncles, Vester and Johnny, helped him learn to play, as did Frank Smith, the new church pastor. Smith later said, "I would show him some runs and different chords . . . That was all: not enough to say I taught him how to play, but I helped him."

The pastor also encouraged Elvis to play the guitar during some of the musical parts of the Sunday church service, and he often saw the boy perform on Saturdays during the amateur portion at the *Jamboree.*

Elvis often took his guitar to school. Sometimes he sang in the classroom, but usually he practiced in the school's basement, which was like a recess area. He was elected to the student council, but many classmates later described Elvis as a loner.

Elvis began learning the guitar at age eleven, when he received one for his birthday.

Some of the students thought Elvis was a trashy boy who played trashy music. In the eighth grade, a gang of boys took his guitar and clipped the strings. Some of the other students chipped in and bought him a new set, though. In 1948, on his last day of junior high school, Elvis gave a going-away concert. The day after, the Presleys moved to Memphis, Tennessee. Elvis was thirteen years old.

The Move to Memphis

Memphis, Tennessee, was a hotbed of rock and roll activity.

"We were broke, man, broke, and we left Tupelo overnight," Elvis said in an interview years later. Memphis was the biggest city in Tennessee at that time. At first, the Presleys could only afford to live in one room in a shabby house. They had to share a bathroom with other families, and there was no kitchen; Gladys cooked the family's meals on a hot plate. After Vernon and Gladys found work, they moved to an apartment in the Lauderdale Courts. Across from the Courts was Shake Rag, a primarily black housing community that was often the site of musical jam sessions.

Gladys asked Jessie Lee Denson, who was two years older than Elvis and the son of the Presleys' preacher, to give her son guitar lessons. The two boys met in the laundry room at the Courts, the only place where they could get some privacy.

Elvis also sang with some boys who performed regularly outside the Courts in the evening, entertaining the neighbors. He would sing often, but his Aunt Lillian remembers Elvis asking her to put out the lights before he would sing at his cousin Bobbie's birthday party. "We had to put out the lights before he'd sing . . . He got way over yonder in the corner—that's just how shy he was," his aunt said.

L. C. Humes High School

Elvis enrolled in L. C. Humes High School. Humes High had 1,600 students—more people than in the entire town of Tupelo. Many of the kids came from poor, white families, like Elvis's. He was an average student who was quiet and obedient and made average grades. Elvis enjoyed English, metal and wood shop, and playing football. He also volunteered at the local library and was in the Reserve Officers' Training Corps (ROTC), a part of the U.S. Army.

Elvis Presley

1934
On January 8, Elvis Aron Presley is born. His twin brother is stillborn.

1944
Elvis sings "Old Shep" at the Mississippi-Alabama Fair and Dairy Show. It is his first public performance.

1948
The Presley family moves to Memphis, Tennessee, and Elvis goes to L. C. Humes High School in Memphis.

1953
Elvis graduates high school in June. He records "My Happiness" and "That's When Your Heartaches Begin" at Sun Studio in August.

1955
Sam Phillips sells Elvis Presley's recording contract to RCA for $40,000. Elvis also performs on *The Steve Allen Show* and does *The Ed Sullivan Show* performance that would make him a household name. In the fall, *Love Me Tender*, Elvis's first movie, premieres in Times Square, New York City.

1958
Elvis Presley is drafted and serves two years in the army. Gladys Presley dies in August.

1967
Elvis and Priscilla Beaulieu are married in a secret Las Vegas wedding ceremony.

1968
Elvis's daughter, Lisa Marie Presley, is born in February. In December, the '68 Comeback Special airs.

1972
Elvis appears in "Elvis: Aloha From Hawaii," the first-ever concert to be broadcast worldwide via satellite. In October, Elvis and Priscilla divorce.

1977
Elvis Presley dies of cardiac arrhythmia in his Graceland mansion on August 16. He is found by his girlfriend, Ginger Alden.

He failed music— "the only thing I ever failed," Elvis said later. His music teacher told him he couldn't sing. He told her that she couldn't appreciate the kind of music that he could sing. The next day, he brought his guitar to class and sang "Keep Them Icy Cold Fingers Off of Me," which was a popular country hit.

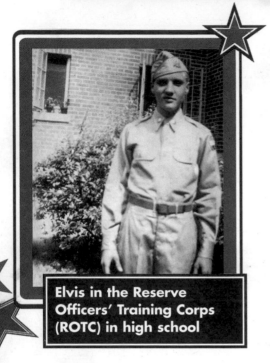

Elvis in the Reserve Officers' Training Corps (ROTC) in high school

The teacher said, "You're right. I don't appreciate your style of music."

High School Graduation

In April 1953, Elvis performed at his high school's annual talent show and was the only one asked for an encore. "It was amazing how popular I became after that," Elvis said later.

The Presleys at Work

In 1950, Vernon hurt his back, and Elvis got jobs at Precision Tool and later at Marl Metal products. He worked after school, from 3:00 to 11:30 PM. But when Elvis fell asleep in the classroom, Gladys told her son to quit his job. She took a job as a nurse's aide at St. Joseph's Hospital. Later, Gladys would cite this job as one of the things she was most proud of.

Elvis went to his senior prom with a girl who had been his neighbor at the Courts. He didn't dance, though, saying he didn't know how. Elvis graduated in 1953 and got a job at the Parker Machinists Shop. He then began working as a truck driver for the Crown Electric Company. While driving, Elvis often passed the Memphis Recording Service, the place that turned his entire life around.

2

"That's All Right"

After World War II, the music
industry enjoyed a unique period
in its history. Mass-produced
record players were more
affordable, and more people owned
them than ever before. That meant
that retail sales of records
were doing big business.
During the war, armed
forces radio had played a
wide variety of music, so
many Americans were
musically open in ways
that they had not
been before. This
also was an era
during which
teenagers had a

great deal of disposable income, and teens started heavily influencing the trends in the entertainment industry.

Television was starting to make its presence felt. During the 1930s, national networks had put on radio shows. Very few of the programs were music programs catering to local audiences. With the advent of national television networks in the 1950s, such as NBC and CBS, the radio shows came to rely more on prerecorded music and on local news and local talent.

Dewey Phillips's first radio show, *Red Hot and Blue*, aired in 1949 on WHBQ, and it became the most popular radio show in Memphis. Dewey played Mississippi-style Delta blues on his show, and the really grungy music was an instant hit with white teenagers. Memphis, Tennessee, at that time led the nation in black radio programming. It was the first place where there was a radio station that played nothing but black R & B.

Several other events happened to shape the birth of rock and roll as we know it. One was the invention of the electric guitar. Another was pop music star Patti Page's sound recording techniques for vocal harmonies. Then there was Atlantic Records's marketing of R & B that had been toned down for white audiences. All of these created a musical climate for a young Elvis Presley, straight out of high school and hungry for making music.

"I Don't Sound Like Nobody"

Sam Phillips and Marion Keisker owned and operated the Memphis Recording Service, which was also known as Sun Records. Phillips and Keisker started the company in 1950. They were known as experts in recording the best of black music. Sam Phillips recorded many black artists who went on to become famous, among them blues great B. B. King.

In August 1953, eighteen-year-old Elvis Presley walked into the Memphis Recording Service carrying the guitar he'd gotten for his eleventh birthday. In the interviews that he gave later, he said he'd gone to the studio to surprise his mother or to hear what he sounded like. However, he could have paid a quarter to make a record at the drugstore to give to his mother or to hear his voice. At that time, in addition to jukeboxes and soda counters where kids could hang out and listen to music with their friends, drugstores often had small recording booths similar to the ones you might see at a county fair. These recording booths weren't as professional as getting a recording done at Sun Studio, where a sound engineer could mix the sound levels to ensure a great recording. Elvis was smart. He wanted to have a record made in a place that had been in the newspaper for producing songs that were exciting the music industry.

In a 1970 interview, Marion Keisker said, "We had a conversation, which I had reason to remember for many, many years afterwards, having gone through it with every editor that I tried to talk to during the time that I was promoting him for Sun."

Marion asked Elvis, "What kind of a singer are you?" "I sing all kinds," Elvis said. She asked him, "Who do you sound like?" "I don't sound like nobody," he answered.

Sam Phillips *(second from left)*, who had recorded the likes of B. B. King, was the first to give Elvis a shot at making records.

Elvis recorded two songs that day: "My Happiness" and "That's When Your Heartaches Begin." Sam Phillips told Elvis that he might call him sometime. Marion Keisker, however, made a note beside Elvis's name: Good ballad singer. Elvis stopped by the studio once in a while to see whether they needed singers for session recordings or demo tapes. Marion was always very nice to Elvis, but there was never any singing work for him to do.

First Love: Dixie Locke

Elvis met Dixie Locke at the First Assembly of God Church. They were crazy about each other and were together all the time. Gladys liked Dixie a lot, too, and it was Gladys's dearest wish that Elvis and Dixie would get married. Although Elvis and Dixie were very much in love, and they often went to concerts or sang together, Elvis did not tell Dixie that he planned to be a musician. Dixie and Elvis went to many radio broadcasts and to all-night performances sponsored by the Blackwood Brothers. They went to WMPS to catch programs by DJ Bob Neal, who later would become Elvis's manager. Elvis wanted to join the Songfellows, a gospel group at his church, but there was no opening for him in the band. Elvis continued to stop by the Memphis Recording Service to see Marion Keisker. He was confident that something would happen. In June 1954, something did.

"Without You"

Sam Phillips had gotten a demo recording of a song, "Without You," from a Nashville promoter. Phillips felt that, with the right singer, the song could be a hit. Marion Keisker urged Sam Phillips to call Elvis Presley.

Elvis went to the Memphis Recording Service and sang the song, also strumming on the guitar. He couldn't seem to get the song right. He was frustrated, but Sam Phillips asked Elvis, "What can you sing?"

Elvis told Phillips the same thing he had told Marion Keisker—that he could sing anything. Then he sang little pieces of all of the songs he knew. Phillips was impressed with the boy's musical range and the naked emotion in Elvis's voice. Sam Phillips introduced Elvis to Scotty Moore, the guitarist for a hillbilly band, the Starlite Wranglers. Sam Phillips suggested that Moore and Bill Black, bassist for the Starlite Wranglers, come to the studio with Elvis. Phillips liked what he heard, and the trio started coming to Sun Studio every day to rehearse after they got

Elvis and Dixie Locke, his high school sweetheart, at her prom

off work. It wasn't long before they recorded a song together, called "That's All Right (Mama)."

Red Hot and Blue

Sam Phillips gave a copy of "That's All Right (Mama)" to Dewey Phillips. Dewey loved the song, and two days later he played the record on his radio show. Elvis was too nervous to listen to it. He went to the movies instead.

After the broadcast, forty-seven calls came in to the station right away, lighting up the switchboard. Dewey called the Presley household to interview Elvis. As the story goes, Vernon and Gladys went down the aisles of the movie theatre until they located Elvis. Within minutes, he was at the station, nervous for what was to come.

First Dewey asked the young singer where he'd gone to high school. Phillips did that because Elvis's answer would tell the listening audience whether he was white or black since schools were segregated at the time. Many of the listeners had thought that the singer of "That's All Right (Mama)" was black.

Did You Know?

The Elvis stamp was released on January 8, 1993, with ceremonies at Graceland. It is the top-selling commemorative postage stamp of all time. The United States Postal Service printed 500 million of them, three times the usual print run for a commemorative stamp. Several other countries have also issued Elvis Presley stamps.

Sam Phillips knew that he had a hit on his hands and that he had to release the record quickly. There was an A-side, which was the hit side, and now they needed a B-side. They recorded "Blue Moon of Kentucky."

By the end of July, the record was number three on the local music sales chart. *Billboard* magazine gave it a positive review. The boys called themselves the Blue Moon Boys, and they began doing live appearances around Memphis.

The Overton Park Show: Fans Go Wild

Elvis spent time with Dixie and continued to work for Crown Electric. There were also the rehearsals at Scotty's house. Vernon advised his son to keep his job at Crown Electric. Vernon thought guitar players were worthless.

Then Elvis was scheduled to appear at the Overton Park Show, opening up for the country singing star Slim Whitman. The crowd reacted wildly to Elvis's stage presence. Scotty Moore quit the Starlite Wranglers. Elvis quit Crown Electric and joined the musicians' union. The band hired Bob Neal as the group's manager. Everyone was eager to see what would happen next, and just how far Elvis could take his success.

3

"Good Rockin' Tonight"

By 1956, rock and roll had been established as a musical form. Rock and roll was a fusion of blues and country music, with an emphasis on a big beat (for a while the music was called the Big Beat). In addition, the imagery of such loud music was reinforced by the lyrical content, which often included fast cars, young love, and rebellion.

Both the sound and the soul of rock and roll gelled from a series of events that happened throughout 1955. Fats Domino recorded the single "Ain't It a Shame." Fats Domino had no less than fifty-nine hits on the R & B charts throughout the fifties, thirty-seven of those hits reaching the Top 40 charts. Pat Boone recorded Domino's song as "Ain't That a Shame." Pat Boone appeared regularly on Arthur Godfrey's popular television show, and that helped to raise public awareness of rock and roll, but it took Elvis Presley to begin the rock and roll revolution.

Audiences Meet the Blue Moon Boys

In October 1954, Sam Phillips drove the Blue Moon Boys to Nashville, Tennessee, to appear on the *Grand Ole Opry*, a famous radio program that launched country music superstars Loretta Lynn and Patsy Cline, among others. Elvis was very nervous before the band's performance, and it happened that the live audience didn't like the Blue Moon Boys. The audience liked traditional country music. The show's host, Jim Denny, swore that the Blue Moon Boys would never again appear on his show.

They had more success on the *Louisiana Hayride*, a program that broadcast from Shreveport, Louisiana. The program was more experimental than the *Grand Old Opry*. Hank Williams got his start on the *Louisiana Hayride*. The audience was younger and more open to new music, and they quickly became fans of the Blue Moon Boys. Elvis was asked to become a regular on the show. That meant he would be appearing there every Saturday night for one year. One of the songs that Elvis sang on the show was Chuck Berry's "Maybellene."

In addition to providing a salary for the up-and-coming musicians, the *Louisiana Hayride* also introduced Elvis to some important people. He met D. J. Fontana, who played with Elvis on the program and who would later become a regular part of Elvis's band. Elvis also met "Colonel" Tom Parker. The Colonel had managed such famous clients as country music star Eddy Arnold.

37

Working Hard

Elvis's second single, "Good Rockin' Tonight," was making its way up the Memphis charts. It got to number three on the charts, and *Billboard* magazine gave it a good review, but it didn't do well outside of Memphis. The B-side of this single was a version of "I Don't Care If the Sun Don't Shine," a song made popular by Dean Martin. By putting a bluesy, country song on one side and a popular tune on the other side, Sam Phillips showed his continued commitment to pairing different musical styles.

Sam Phillips was more convinced than ever that he had found a kindred spirit in Elvis Presley, both musically and in the mission of promoting black R & B. Sam Phillips said, "The lack of prejudice on the part of Elvis Presley had to be one of the biggest things that ever could have happened to us, though. It was almost subversive, sneaking around through the music. . ."

It is interesting that Sam Phillips had so much faith in Elvis's lack of prejudice. In later years, critics of Elvis would charge him with stealing the thunder of rock and roll from black performers. These were, critics maintained, the true pioneers of rock and roll. Some critics also believed that these true pioneers were never credited properly by Elvis.

On Tour

The band continued to tour the South and the Southwest. Sometimes audiences loved what Elvis was doing, and sometimes they were hostile. Many young men didn't like how their girlfriends screamed and went crazy over the sexy young singer. Elvis was a quick learner. He refined his stage persona at every performance, through trial and error. If the audience went wild for one of his movements, Elvis remembered it and worked it into the act again.

Elvis loved shopping, and he carefully chose his onstage wardrobe. His favorite colors were pink and black. Elvis bought his clothes at Lansky's on Beale Street in Memphis. He bought a striped sports coat with a velvet collar. Guy Lansky recalled later that Elvis loved it so much that he kept it for many years after he had first bought it.

Elvis made enough money for manager Bob Neal to set up the band's offices in Memphis. Neal started an Elvis Presley fan club and ordered stationery in pink and black. Elvis bought cool cars, among them a pink Ford and a pink Cadillac. Still, Elvis continued to tour as one of the opening acts for more established performers and to rehearse when he was in Memphis. More and more often, Elvis stole the show whenever he performed.

Fun Fact!

The name "Elvis" is taken from the Scandinavian name "Alviss," meaning "all wise." His middle name, Aron, is from the Bible. Elvis's middle name was spelled with one a on his birth certificate but with two a's on his tombstone. Some think this is a sign that Elvis is still alive.

"I'm Left, You're Right, She's Gone"

Dixie was beginning to find out more and more that she just didn't fit into Elvis's new life. They still cared for each other, and Dixie spent a lot of time with Gladys Presley when Elvis was away on tour. But Dixie and Elvis fought a lot,

Although Elvis's middle name is spelled "Aron" on his birth certificate, his tombstone reads "Aaron."

mostly about what Dixie was doing when Elvis was away. Elvis was very possessive, and he wanted Dixie to sit at home and wait for him instead of going to the drugstore to listen to some music with her friends. Dixie suspected that Elvis dated other girls, and she was right, although there was no one else who was steady or serious with Elvis at this time but Dixie. They had broken up a few times, and in July 1955, they broke up for good.

Elvis did not let his personal life interfere with his music, however. Elvis's fourth Sun single paired an R & B tune, "Baby, Let's Play House," with a country tune, "I'm Left, You're Right, She's Gone." This record sold incredibly well, and Elvis Presley became a household name throughout the South.

The group had been saving money for a trip to New York City to audition for Arthur Godfrey's popular television show. When they got to New York, the woman who ran the auditions did not like Elvis's music, and the band never appeared on the show. They continued to tour, and they made enough money so that Elvis could rent a house for himself and his parents.

Girls Go Crazy for Elvis!

Elvis appeared in a tour opening for country singers Hank Snow and Slim Whitman, among others. It was Colonel Parker's influence that got Elvis on this tour, since Elvis was not exactly a country singer. Part of Elvis's appeal was that he couldn't be so easily classified, and therefore he could fit into many different musical slots with the right marketing.

Girls in the audience often went wild at the very sight of Elvis Presley.

Parker had been helping Bob Neal to book shows for Elvis, even though Neal was still Elvis's official manager. From the start, this tour was different. People were beginning to recognize the exciting young singer; Elvis was becoming something more than a novelty or a local act.

This tour was also the beginning of what would become par for the course at Elvis Presley concerts—the fans were causing riots wherever he

Fans reach desperately for "the King," Elvis Presley.

appeared. A perfect example of the kind of attention Elvis would come to command happened in Jacksonville, Florida. Onstage, Elvis announced, "Girls, I'll see you all backstage," and the eager fans rushed the stage, grabbing for Elvis's clothes and ripping them before he got away.

It was this incident that convinced Colonel Parker to manage Elvis Presley. Their association did not begin right away because Bob Neal was still managing Elvis, and his contract had not run out yet. Another reason was that Gladys Presley didn't like the Colonel. The Colonel wooed the Presleys and bided his time. Parker knew he could launch Elvis's career into the big time.

"Mystery Train"

When Elvis got back to Memphis, he went into Sun Studio to record. The first single he recorded was "I Forgot to Remember to Forget." This was the song that established Elvis's popularity in the country and western market. The B-side was "Mystery Train." "Mystery Train" reached number one on the country charts in November 1955. It was the last single that Elvis recorded for Sun.

4

Elvis on the Rise

Elvis worked every weekend on the *Louisiana Hayride*, toured, and sought publicity. Colonel Parker tried to get the major record label RCA interested in signing Elvis to a record deal. The Colonel intended to be the boy's manager when Elvis's contract was up with Bob Neal.

The Colonel booked Elvis for the Hank Snow and Bill Haley tour. This would bring important publicity for Elvis. Bill Haley said of Elvis: "He had the attitude which most young kids do that he was really going to go out there and stop the show and knock Bill Haley off the stage, which at that time was an impossibility, because we were number one . . . When I came back after doing my show he was kind of half crying in the dressing room, very downhearted . . . and I told him, 'Look, you got a lot of talent.'"

Elvis was the main attraction in his own right at a lot of shows. In west Texas, Johnny Cash was one of the opening acts for Elvis. In Lubbock, Texas, Buddy Holly, who went on to be a big rock and roll star, opened for Elvis.

Good-Bye to Sun

Sam Phillips wasn't sure whether he should sell Elvis's contract. He didn't want Sun Studio to be known only as the studio that recorded Elvis Presley. Sam was excited about working with Carl Perkins. Carl Perkins was one of the first musicians who was directly influenced by Elvis Presley's sound and who tried to copy it.

In 1955, the Presleys and Colonel Parker signed a "special adviser" contract. Colonel Parker, who was a special adviser while Bob Neal was still manager, got record companies to compete over buying Elvis's record contract from Sun. RCA was the Colonel's first choice, partly because he had connections there. RCA had good television and movie connections, too. Elvis was eager to be a movie star.

Sam Phillips sold Elvis's recording contract to RCA for $40,000. Sam Phillips received $35,000 and $5,000 went to Elvis. Because RCA had spent so much money for Elvis Presley's contract, the company would do whatever it took to promote him.

The Man Behind Elvis Presley: Colonel Tom Parker

Colonel Tom Parker was born Andreas van Kuijk in the Netherlands and arrived in America in 1929, enlisting in the U.S. Army as Andre van Kuijk. That he could get into the army without a birth certificate showed the Colonel's persuasive abilities, which later would be useful to him in

Elvis with his manager
Colonel Tom Parker, and his
mother, Gladys

selling his "product," Elvis Presley. Still, some say
that it was because the Colonel was in the
country illegally that Elvis never toured outside
of the United States.

When he got out of the army, he
changed his name to Tom Parker and worked
in carnivals and as a "chief dogcatcher," he told

people later. In 1948, the governor of Louisiana gave Tom Parker an honorary title of "colonel."

Elvis said of his relationship with the Colonel: "We're the perfect combination. The Colonel's an old carny, and me, I'm off the wall."

Recording at RCA

In 1956, two days after Elvis's twenty-first birthday, he first recorded at the RCA studios. Chet Atkins, guitar rock legend, coproduced this session with Steve Sholes, the RCA vice president who had signed Elvis. Everyone was nervous. Elvis needed to record great records that would rocket to the top of the charts and bring in lots of money.

Two of the songs recorded would go on to be some of Elvis's most memorable: "Heartbreak Hotel" and "I Was the One." "Heartbreak Hotel" was a sort of a gloomy song, and Steve Sholes wasn't sure about releasing it as Elvis's first RCA single. He did, though, and the public loved it. It quickly climbed into the national Top 40 chart, and television offers started to pour in.

Stage Show and the First Television Appearances

Elvis's first television appearances were on *Stage Show,* hosted by the big-band leaders Jimmy and Tommy Dorsey. Television was the medium that would launch Elvis's career. More people would see him on one television show than at all of the concerts he could do in a tour. One of the songs that Elvis sang on the show was Little Richard's "Tutti Frutti."

Elvis called his parents every day, no matter where he was. He was worried about his mother, who had not been in the best of health. He knew that Gladys worried about him, and he called to reassure her.

On the road again, it was clear that television had provided a great boost to Elvis Presley's star appeal. However, the grueling schedule was too much for Elvis: He collapsed before a show in Jacksonville, Florida, and was hospitalized for exhaustion for one night.

Elvis sang "Heartbreak Hotel" and "Blue Suede Shoes," a tune that Carl Perkins had recorded for Sun, on the last of his Dorsey TV appearances. "Blue Suede Shoes" was competing for popularity with "Heartbreak Hotel" on the music charts. "Heartbreak Hotel," by the end of March 1956, had sold close to a million copies, and it was nearly at the top of all three music charts: pop, country, and rhythm and blues. No other artist, or single, had managed such a sweeping success. Also, Elvis's first full album recorded for RCA would become the label's first million-dollar album. It was around this time, in March 1956, that Elvis Presley signed the contract making Colonel Parker his manager.

Hooray for Hollywood

Elvis had a screen test with Hal Wallis, who had made the *Maltese Falcon* and *Casablanca*. Elvis wanted to be a serious actor, like Marlon Brando or James Dean. He wasn't interested in just singing in the movies. However, his first screen test included him miming some songs with a toy guitar. Everyone at the studio was impressed with the energy that Elvis had

Did You Know?

Elvis's style began to take shape early in his life. During his junior year of high school, Elvis was kicked off the football team for refusing to cut his hair! He wore dressy pants and shirts, snazzy shoes, and flashy sports jackets.

when he was holding a guitar, even a toy one, in his hands: "The electricity just bounced off the walls of the sound stage," screenwriter Alan Weiss said. Elvis was signed to a three-movie contract with 20th Century Fox.

Elvis appeared on *The Milton Berle Show* in 1956 for the first time. He sang "Heartbreak Hotel" and "Blue Suede Shoes." A comedy sketch featured Milton Berle in an outfit identical to Elvis's, with his pants rolled up like a hillybilly's and sporting enormous blue suede shoes. He introduced himself as Elvis's twin brother, Melvin. If Elvis was upset about the reference to a twin brother, he did not show it.

"Hound Dog," Las Vegas, and Steve Allen

Elvis's two-week appearance at the New Frontier hotel in Las Vegas bombed. The fans in Las Vegas were older, and they did not like rock and roll. In Las Vegas, Elvis heard a band performing "Hound Dog," first recorded by blues singer Big Mama Thornton in 1953. It was a song that would become one of Elvis's most famous recordings.

Milton Berle and Elvis on *The Milton Berle Show*

Elvis appeared again on *The Milton Berle Show* and performed "Hound Dog." Elvis's outrageous performance and his sexy dance

Elvis performed to a live hound dog on *The Steve Allen Show*.

moves provoked a big reaction from parents and critics.

Elvis appeared next on *The Steve Allen Show*. Steve Allen did not like rock and roll. He insisted that Presley appear wearing a tuxedo and blue suede shoes, and he made Elvis stand still. Elvis appeared onstage alone, singing to a real-live hound dog.

Elvis fans picketed in front of the television studio with signs that read, "We want the real Elvis!" This made Ed Sullivan, the host of the popular *The Ed Sullivan Show*, book Elvis Presley. Sullivan offered Elvis $50,000, three times the money that Ed Sullivan had ever offered anyone.

June Juanico and Fans Everywhere Love Elvis

When Elvis went back into the studio in Memphis, he recorded "Hound Dog" and "Don't Be Cruel." Then he took three weeks of vacation. He was dating June Juanico, a beauty queen from Biloxi, Mississippi. She wasn't the only girl he was dating. Elvis's career was his priority and he did not want to settle down. He never let his romances get too intimate because he had an image to protect. His career would suffer from any scandal about girls.

At home in Memphis, Elvis signed autographs for hours every day, a practice that he would keep up for life. Elvis's fame meant that he was rarely alone. Fans on the street mobbed him. At his Fourth of July concert in Memphis in 1956—the day was renamed Elvis Presley Day by the mayor of the city—the crowd was so loud that it was said that extra sleeping pills were given to patients in the nearby hospitals.

Elvis Presley performed live on *The Ed Sullivan Show* for $50,000, three times what any other act had ever received up to that time.

The Ed Sullivan Show

Elvis Presley's three appearances on *The Ed Sullivan Show* in 1956 made him a rock and roll superstar. The press called him Elvis the Pelvis. Because so many people were shocked by Elvis's dance moves, for his last appearance on the show, in January 1957, the singer was filmed only from the waist up. Elvis wiggled his eyebrows and his shoulders as he sang, and crooked his little finger to suggest the banned dance movies. The fans went bananas.

The Ed Sullivan Show appearances were so successful that Colonel Parker decided he would demand an extremely high price for Elvis to make TV appearances. Elvis did not appear on television again until 1960. This was in part because Elvis was ready for the next step: He was going to be a movie star.

5

"Jailhouse Rock"

Elvis arrived in Hollywood in August 1956. He would get $100,000 for his first movie, $150,000 for the second, and $200,000 for the third. Although these were high figures for an untried actor, the profits from Elvis's movies would average ten times these amounts.

The first movie was

a western called *Love Me Tender,* after the ballad that Elvis recorded for the movie's sound track. Unlike Elvis's later movies, this one has few songs in it.

Love Me Tender premiered at the Paramount Theater in Times Square, New York, and there was a forty-foot Elvis cutout looming above the movie marquee. The Colonel swam through the crowd, handing out "Elvis for President" buttons. The national release that followed was the largest one in the history of 20th Century Fox. The movie got bad reviews but did well at the box office.

To get an idea of how much Elvis's career shifted when he started doing movies, consider that he did 200 concerts in 1955. He did more than one hundred live performances in 1956, and he performed eleven times on television. In 1957, after his movie career started, Elvis performed only twenty concerts and did one television appearance. And, after more than two years and nine hit singles, Elvis was about to be drafted!

Elvis's first film was a western called *Love Me Tender*, which included his song of the same name.

Military Stirrings and *Loving You*

Elvis was eligible for the draft in 1957. After the pre-induction physical, he filmed his second movie. The movie title was *Loving You,* after a song on the sound track. The movie was loosely based on Elvis's career.

Before the movie was shot, Elvis went into a Los Angeles studio to record gospel songs for a religious album, as well as the single "All Shook Up." Elvis's parents flew out to Hollywood, and Gladys and Vernon can be seen as extras in one scene of *Loving You*.

After the movie wrapped and before filming his third movie, Elvis Presley bought the Graceland mansion in Memphis for $102,500. He paid almost as much to remodel it. Elvis wanted an eight-foot-square bed, a fifteen-foot sofa, a soda fountain, a chicken coop in the backyard for his mother, and a swimming pool. Graceland's gate featured musical notes and two guitar-playing Elvises. Elvis would always call Graceland home, although he later bought other houses.

Jailhouse Rock

"Shake, Rattle and Roll," a big hit for Bill Haley, was written by Jerry Leiber and Mike Stoller. They wrote many great songs, such as "Hound Dog," "Love Potion No. 9," "Stand by Me,"

Jailhouse Rock is widely considered to be one of Elvis Presley's best films.

"Chapel of Love," "Jailhouse Rock," and "Treat Me Nice." The Beatles were avid fans of Leiber and Stoller's songs.

Leiber and Stoller composed most of the sound track for *Jailhouse Rock*. Many people consider *Jailhouse Rock* Elvis's best movie. The film features Scotty Moore, Bill Black, and D. J. Fontana as Elvis's band, although the band broke up not long after *Jailhouse Rock* was released.

Elvis's 1957 single, "Teddy Bear," vied for the top spot on the charts with Jerry Lee Lewis's "Whole Lotta Shakin' Goin' On." Fans sent thousands of teddy bears to Graceland. Elvis gave most of them to charity. He was active in many charities throughout his life.

The Army

Elvis's draft notice came just before Christmas 1957. Although he put on a brave face for his family and friends, Elvis did not want to go into the army. He followed the Colonel's advice to the letter, though, and if the Colonel thought Elvis should serve in the army, that's what Elvis would do. Elvis could have served in the entertainment corps. The entertainment corps are groups of entertainers who enlist in the armed forces but who, instead of training for the military, spend their service time rehearsing for and performing shows to entertain the troops. However, the Colonel thought Elvis should prove that he could be a soldier. Elvis delayed his army entrance to shoot the movie *King Creole*. *King Creole* was Elvis's favorite of all of his movies.

After shooting the movie, Elvis palled around with friends in Memphis. He arrived at the draft board with carloads of friends, his parents, then-girlfriend Anita,

Fun Fact!

During the filming of *Jailhouse Rock*, Elvis aspirated (breathed in) one of the porcelain caps from his teeth and it lodged in his lung. He had to be hospitalized to remove the cap. In fact, this accident mirrored one of the events in the film!

Instead of a cushy gig in the entertainment corps, Elvis underwent basic training during his time in the U.S. Army.

and the Colonel. As Elvis said good-bye, Colonel Parker handed out *King Creole* balloons. Gladys Presley wept openly.

Elvis boarded a bus for Fort Chaffee, Arkansas. For Elvis's first few army days, the press photographed everything he did. Army officials even chased a photographer out of the barracks for trying to get a photo of Elvis sleeping on an army cot! The press was on hand to photograph Elvis's regulation army haircut. Elvis smiled for the cameras. He joked, "Hair today, gone tomorrow."

Elvis was assigned to the Second Armored Division at Fort Hood, outside Killeen, Texas. Private Elvis Presley did well as a soldier, winning marksman and sharpshooter medals, and acting as the assistant squad leader.

After basic training, Elvis spent two weeks at Graceland. He wore his uniform because he was proud of it. RCA released Elvis's first greatest-hits album and his twenty-second single. *King Creole* opened in theaters to excellent reviews. Finally, Elvis did a recording session for RCA.

Gladys Presley's Death

Vernon, Gladys, and Grandma Minnie Mae lived in a rented house in Killeen, Texas, near the army base. Private Presley could live with his parents instead of on the base because they were his dependents. Gladys Presley had a weak heart, and her hepatitis, a liver ailment, was made worse by her abuse of diet pills and alcohol. Elvis asked for leave to see her when she was hospitalized, and the army reluctantly let him go. In August 1958, Gladys passed away.

Back at Graceland for the funeral, Elvis told reporters, "She's all we lived for. She was always my best girl." Elvis grieved for weeks. He returned to Fort Hood after an extended leave.

Moving to Germany

Private Presley traveled by train to New York and boarded a ship for West Germany. In New York, there was a press conference with the Colonel in attendance. A band played "Tutti Frutti" as Elvis walked up the ship's gangplank.

Elvis's records sold well in Germany, and there was a crowd waiting for him when he landed. There was a three-day open house for the press at his post, but then the press left him alone, on army orders. Elvis was a scout jeep driver. He lived off base with Vernon and Grandma Minnie Mae in a house that had a sign posted: "Autographs Between 7:30 and 8:30 PM."

Elvis worried that his fans would forget him, but the Colonel worked to ensure Elvis's popularity. Elvis got as many as 10,000 fan letters a week. RCA

Young Elvis fell in love with Priscilla Beaulieu during his stay in Germany.

worried that there wasn't enough material to last throughout Elvis's army stay, even though they were releasing the already-recorded singles slowly. There were no Elvis Presley songs on *Billboard*'s Hot 100 chart in 1959, for the first time in almost three years. The company repackaged old material. The Colonel announced that the first movie Elvis would make when he got out of the army would be *G.I. Blues,* based on his experiences in the army.

Learning Karate and Meeting Priscilla

Life was not all dreary in Germany or in the army. Elvis became interested in karate; later in life he became a black belt. He also became smitten with fourteen-year-old Priscilla Beaulieu, the daughter of an air force officer.

In 1960, shortly after Elvis was promoted to sergeant, he was discharged a month early. The Colonel immediately rereleased *Jailhouse Rock*. RCA made the decision to press a million copies of Elvis's first post-army single, even before the single had been recorded! Elvis's first TV appearance after leaving the army would be on *The Frank Sinatra Show*. Elvis would receive $125,000 for the appearance. It was more money than any other TV appearance had ever commanded.

At a press conference in Germany, Elvis saw Marion Keisker, from Sun Studio, who was a captain in the air force. "What do I do? Kiss you, or salute you?" Elvis asked. "In that order," she told him. Elvis told the newsmen the part Keisker had played in his career. She was very touched; it was the first time he had publicly acknowledged her part in his musical success.

There are photos of Priscilla waving good-bye to Elvis at the airport. However, those

A staged publicity photo of Priscilla waving good-bye to Elvis.

photos were taken the day after Elvis left. The pictures were staged for publicity, to be published in magazines. Elvis and Priscilla really said their good-byes privately. They promised to write to each other.

Starting with the letters they wrote before Priscilla went to live at Graceland, Elvis and Priscilla's courtship would last for eight years, culminating in marriage and then divorce. As the mother of Elvis's child, she was queen to his king in a way no one else was, though Elvis openly cheated on her during their marriage.

After his army experience in Germany, Elvis went back to America, anxious to see whether he could pick up his career where he had left off.

The Downward Spiral

6

In 1960, Elvis had served in the army for two years, but he jumped right back into his career. There was an RCA recording session, a guest appearance on *Frank Sinatra's Welcome Home Party for Elvis Presley* television special, and the filming of *G.I. Blues*. Elvis resumed his relationship with Anita, as well as with Elisabeth, his personal secretary in Germany who followed him to Graceland.

There had been some newcomers in the music industry since Elvis had been away. After his 1958 hit "Splish Splash," Bobby Darin had won a Grammy Award in 1959 for "Mack the Knife." Also, many of Elvis's rock and roll contemporaries were no longer on the scene. Jerry Lee Lewis had retired because of a sex scandal. Buddy Holly and Ritchie Valens had died in a plane crash. Little Richard had become a minister.

Elvis had three number-one singles in a row in 1960: "Stuck on You," "Now or Never," and "Are You Lonesome Tonight?" His popularity was undiminished, but two of these three songs were ballads. Where was the hard-rocking Elvis Presley?

When Elvis got back to Nashville, he went into the recording studio and recorded the album *Elvis Is Back*. The album quickly zoomed to number one on the charts. Next, Elvis went to Hollywood to film *G.I. Blues*. Most of the music in this movie is pop music. The film got poor reviews but was a smash success at the box office.

Priscilla at Graceland

Vernon married Dee Stanley, a woman he had met in Germany, and moved out of Graceland into a small house nearby. The young Priscilla Beaulieu moved into Graceland shortly afterward. Elvis was crazy about Priscilla. He gave her

Elvis's first film after the military was *G.I. Blues*, based on his army career.

anything she wanted. He enrolled her in a private Catholic girls' high school. She graduated in 1963.

Elvis taught Priscilla to be his ideal woman. He chose her wardrobe, and she dyed her hair jet black to match his, wearing it in a complicated beehive. This did not mean that Elvis stopped seeing other girls, however.

Grammy Awards and Movie Mania

Elvis received several Grammy nominations in 1960 for "Are You Lonesome Tonight?" and the *G.I. Blues* album. He had a stack of gold records and recorded *His Hand in Mine,* an album of inspirational music. He also sang at a benefit concert in Hawaii in 1961. He would not perform publicly again for seven years.

Blue Hawaii was made while he was on location in Hawaii. Like many of his post-army movies, it is silly but harmless. These movies and the image of Elvis as a family-style entertainer represented quite a departure from his beginnings as a rock and roll rebel.

Elvis made twenty-six movies in the time from *Blue Hawaii* in 1961 to *Change of Habit* in 1969. He made thirty-three films in all; however, not one of these movies showcased Elvis in the dramatic role he longed to do. The films seemed to be showcases for uninspired popular music sold as movie sound tracks to keep the money coming in.

In the 1972 documentary film *Elvis on Tour*, Elvis said, "At a certain stage, I had no say-so in it. I didn't have final approval on the script, which means that I couldn't tell you, 'This is not good for me' . . . I don't think anyone was consciously trying to harm me. It was just Hollywood's image of me was wrong, and I knew it, and I couldn't say anything about it, couldn't do anything about it . . . I really took it as long as I could."

Viva Las Vegas

One of the bright spots of the moviemaking period was *Viva Las Vegas*, filmed in 1963 with sexy costar Ann-Margret, who had been in the box-office hit *'Bye 'Bye, Birdie*, a rock and roll musical based loosely on Elvis's career and stint in the army. Many felt that Ann-Margret was one of the only costars Elvis ever had who could match him in talent and sex appeal. It was also said that the reason why Ann-Margret and Elvis never worked together again is because the Colonel was nervous about anyone who could potentially outshine his star client.

The '60s Music Scene and Elvis: An Overview

Consider what was going on in the music scene during the 1960s: Rock music was experimental and grungy with the likes of Lou Reed and the Velvet Underground. The hippie subculture and folk rock existed alongside psychedelic rock. These forms took root and culminated in the Monterey and Altamont pop festivals, with groups such as the Grateful Dead and artists such as Jimi Hendrix and Janis Joplin. Then there were rock groups as different as the Doors and the Beach Boys. Don't forget Marvin Gaye and other Motown artists doing great soul music.

Where would Elvis Presley fit into this music scene? Elvis was concentrating on making movies during the sixties. The music he recorded was mainly for movie sound tracks. However, during these moviemaking years, he was Hollywood's top box-office draw and one of the highest-paid actors in America. Also, some of his best-selling music came from movie sound tracks. Eleven of his movie sound tracks went to the top ten on the music charts. Of those, four went to number one, among them *G.I. Blues* and *Blue Hawaii.*

Elvis and Ann-Margret had a steamy affair off-screen as well as a lot of chemistry onscreen. Priscilla first became suspicious and then furious when she read the reports in the papers about Elvis's affair with Ann-Margret. Elvis was aware

Ann-Margret and Elvis Presley seemed to hit it off very well, both onscreen and off.

that he had persuaded Priscilla's parents to let her come to Graceland with the understanding that he wanted to marry her, but he still didn't want to give up his bachelor lifestyle.

Taking Stock

Elvis Presley was thirty in 1965, and Colonel Tom Parker had been managing Elvis's career for ten years. Elvis had made seventeen movies, which had grossed about $130 million, and he had sold a hundred million records, which had made $150 million. His fans were still loyal, but whereas once Elvis had such a following because he was an artistic pioneer, the tune had changed. Perhaps the loyalty of Elvis's fans was keeping his career afloat.

Even though Elvis may have wanted to try something new in his career, it wasn't easy. Colonel Parker encouraged Elvis to stick with material that would appeal to the broadest possible audience. Also, Elvis didn't always record with the same group, so it was difficult to have creative support. Finally, Elvis did not write his

Did You Know?

Elvis had a group of friends called the Memphis Mafia. They all wore dark suits and sunglasses. They traveled with Elvis everywhere in an official capacity as his bodyguards or accountants, but really because Elvis couldn't stand to be alone.

own songs, as the Beatles did, so he couldn't reinvent his music firsthand.

Married at Last

Priscilla Beaulieu married Elvis Presley in 1967. It was a Las Vegas wedding, kept secret for as long as possible. Elvis and Priscilla arrived in Las Vegas in the middle of the night and went straight to the Clark County courthouse for the marriage license. From there they went to the Aladdin Hotel, where, after a few hours of rest, they were married in a suite of the hotel later that morning.

The ceremony was performed by a Nevada Supreme Court judge and lasted for eight minutes. Priscilla's ring had a three-carat diamond and twenty smaller ones, and she wore a white chiffon dress with a six-foot train. The groom was in a black tuxedo. The judge said, "Elvis . . . was low-key, handsome

Priscilla and Elvis Presley with their daughter, Lisa Marie, who was born on February 1, 1968

as a picture, very respectful and very intense . . . and so nervous he was almost bawling." Exactly nine months after the wedding, on February 1, 1968, Lisa Marie Presley was born.

Back on the Road to Creativity

Elvis wanted out of his movie career. He had accepted the Colonel's business advice because he believed that the Colonel was his good-luck charm. Elvis knew that the entertainment industry was changing, and he wanted to change with it. *Stay Away, Joe*, made in 1968, had only three songs. It focused on Elvis's acting, and he hoped it would make the movie industry take him seriously as an actor.

Elvis began to reinvent his sound. Felton Jarvis, the Nashville producer of Elvis's Grammy-winning *How Great Thou Art*, kept Elvis inspired and on-track in the studio. Together, they recorded some fresh new singles, among them "Guitar Man," which, although it didn't even hit the top ten on the music charts, did better on the charts than most of the other music he had done for years.

In early 1968, the Colonel wanted Elvis to do a Christmas special for television. It would be the first time Elvis had appeared on television since 1960 and the first time in years that he had appeared in front of a live audience. NBC had offered to pay Elvis half a million dollars for the special. More important than money was the question, Would this special reestablish Elvis as the king of rock and roll?

7

Elvis, What Happened?

Instead of making a sappy
Christmas special, Elvis decided
to do a strong comeback
special. He wanted to
prove to the public that
he could still rock and
roll. One of the events
that influenced Elvis's
decision took place on
the Sunset Strip, in Los
Angeles. Elvis and the
Memphis Mafia went
for a walk along

the Strip. It had been ten years since Elvis had felt comfortable going out in broad daylight. He was always mobbed by fans. This time, however, Elvis got no attention at all. It was a real wake-up call for the King.

The *'68 Comeback Special* aired in December 1968. Elvis wore a tight black leather suit, and he was thinner than he had been even at the start of his career. Elvis sang everything from material he'd recorded at Sun Studio to the most recent songs. The more mature Elvis Presley vocal style was pitched lower and was beautiful for slower, ballad-style singing. Elvis was simply terrific.

"If I Can Dream"

"If I Can Dream" had been written especially for the *'68 Comeback Special,* and after the special aired, the single shot to number twelve on the music charts. It was his first million-dollar record in three years. The special's sound track climbed the charts to number eight.

Elvis was so excited with this success that he wanted to record music and tour again. However,

Elvis's '68 Comeback Special on television was considered by many to be a triumphant return to form.

he had a contract for three more movies. After these movies, the only Elvis movies that came out were performance documentaries.

Back in the Studio

Elvis went into the recording studio in Memphis and was amazingly productive. He recorded "In the Ghetto," "Suspicious Minds," and "Don't Cry Daddy." They all became number-one singles. Then Elvis went back to touring and performing for live audiences.

Colonel Parker was not too happy with Elvis's decision to do live performances again. They had a big argument. Elvis stuck to his guns, even though the Colonel threatened to quit. The Colonel, in fact, did not quit, and Elvis took to the stage once again.

Las Vegas Concert

Elvis did a four-week engagement at the International Hotel in Las Vegas in July 1968. By the time the Colonel was done refining the contract, Elvis had been signed for a second engagement to follow the first, and he would earn $1 million total. Elvis had two gospel quartets on this tour: the Imperials, a male gospel quartet, and the Sweet Inspirations, a female group (whose leader was Cissy Houston, Whitney Houston's mother).

The fans hadn't liked Elvis when he played in Las Vegas in 1956. This time around, not only did the fans love Elvis during this Las Vegas tour, but the critics did, too. The show got great reviews, and Elvis had brought in more fans than any other Las Vegas performer had, even more than Barbra Streisand.

When the show was over, Elvis took a short vacation, and then he went on the road. Elvis repeated this process for the rest of his career: Las Vegas shows, touring, recording, and vacations.

Strange Days

Elvis's career was going fairly well, but his personal life was getting stranger and stranger, starting in the early 1970s. The Memphis Mafia, many of whom were relatives or childhood friends, catered to his whims. He had a gun collection and shot televisions if he happened to dislike what was on them. He made up for his fits of temper with equally extreme fits of generosity. He might spend $85,000 buying out a jewelry store to present all of his close associates with jewelry. Often the jewelry was inscribed with the letters "TCB," which stood for Elvis's motto: Taking Care of Business. He might spend more than $100,000 buying Cadillacs, Rolls-Royces, Mercedes-Benzes, and the like for friends or even for complete strangers who happened to be in the car showrooms.

Elvis became increasingly dependent on drugs. Elvis was against the use of hard drugs, and he did not approve of drinking or of smoking marijuana. He had started using amphetamines, or speed, to stay awake during guard duty when he was in the army. He continued the practice throughout his life.

Elvis also took diet pills to control his eating habits. He always ate exactly what he wanted, including plenty of burnt bacon, grilled peanut butter sandwiches, and hamburgers. Both amphetamines and diet pills are highly addictive. Finally, Elvis took sleeping pills for his insomnia. Because doctors prescribed the pills, Elvis believed he needed the "medicine" the doctors gave him.

Today, we know how addictive prescription drugs are and how careful doctors must be not to overmedicate patients. At that time, no one recognized how serious the problem was—or had the courage to confront Elvis about it—until it was too late. Elvis Presley's drug dependence was tragic. Drugs undoubtedly cut short his career and his life.

Priscilla and Elvis Split

Priscilla hated the Memphis Mafia and Elvis's touring all the time. Priscilla thought Elvis spoiled Lisa Marie by letting the child do whatever she wanted. Most important, Priscilla was very concerned about Elvis's drug use. Early in 1972, Priscilla left Elvis, taking Lisa Marie with her to California.

Elvis did not understand why Priscilla had left. He was especially hurt because she had left him

Elvis in the '70s: An Overview

It is amazing to think that Elvis shared the 1970s music scene with David Bowie's Ziggy Stardust, Bob Marley's popularization of reggae music, rock supergroups such as Led Zeppelin, and, toward the end of his career, even with the Ramones, the New York Dolls, and the Sex Pistols. Between 1969 and 1977, Elvis performed 1,126 concerts, in addition to performing in Las Vegas for eight weeks each year. Elvis performed in Las Vegas in 1970 and broke all attendance records for concerts at the International Hotel. Elvis toured America throughout the seventies, breaking box-office records wherever he appeared, including a sold-out show at New York's Madison Square Garden in

1972. Of the fourteen Grammy Award nominations that Elvis received during his career, he won four; three of them were awarded to him during the seventies.

for a karate instructor to whom he had introduced her. It is doubtful whether Elvis ever recovered from this blow. It was the main event that set him on a downward spiral. He and Priscilla still remained friends, though. Priscilla went on to become an actress, appearing most notably in the *Naked Gun* movies.

Elvis kept working. He had filmed two performance documentaries, *Elvis: That's the Way It Is* and *Elvis on Tour*. He also toured continually. All of this work couldn't hide the fact that Elvis Presley was terribly depressed. The material that he chose to sing was loaded with sad ballads about lost love.

Back at Work?

In 1973, Elvis appeared in the first-ever live concert broadcast around the world via satellite, *Elvis: Aloha from Hawaii.* Elvis worked hard to get in shape, doing karate and dieting. The costume designer created an all-white jumpsuit that featured a belt set with real rubies. Elvis gave away the belt at the last minute, and the costume designer scrambled to locate enough rubies to create another belt. The concert raised $85,000 for a Hawaiian charity, and Elvis was in top form. Elvis was still depressed, though. Everyone wondered how much longer his career could last.

Elvis recorded again in 1973. Unlike his early recording sessions, during which he would do thirty-six or more takes of a song, this time Elvis was listless and his technique was sloppy. Some days, he didn't show up at all, telling the musicians that he was sick.

That summer he went back to Las Vegas, drawing 100,000 fans to the Vegas Hilton in one month. For this he received more money than any other Vegas entertainer had been paid.

Divorce and Detox, Lawsuits and Luxury Cars

Priscilla and Elvis were divorced in October 1973. Six days later, Elvis checked into a hospital in Memphis for eighteen days, reportedly for the flu but probably to detoxify from Demerol, a painkiller. This was the first of his hospital visits, but not the last.

Elvis's behavior became more erratic. He flew to Washington, D.C., demanding from President Richard Nixon a Federal Bureau of Narcotics badge. Elvis started to collect honorary police badges from many areas in the country.

Elvis also began to say terribly abusive things to his musicians onstage. Musicians quit, even though Elvis often made up for his cruel taunts by buying expensive gifts. Three longtime members of the Memphis Mafia, Red and Sonny West and Dave Hebler, left Elvis and began to write a tell-all book about him with journalist Robert Dunleavy, titled *Elvis, What Happened?*

Also, Elvis was involved in several lawsuits that forced him to reexamine his finances for

Elvis poses for a picture with President Richard Nixon.

the first time in years because he had to make public his earnings. Court documents revealed that, although Elvis had earned $7.25 million in 1974, mostly from touring, he had netted $1.5 million after taxes and expenses and had spent $700,000 on personal rather than business costs.

Did You Know?

In 1986, Elvis was among the first group of inductees into the Rock and Roll Hall of Fame. In 1987, Elvis was honored with the first posthumous presentation of the Award of Merit by the American Music Awards. In 1998, Elvis received the Country Music Association's highest honor, induction into the Country Music Hall of Fame.

The Beginning of the End

As Elvis's fortieth birthday grew closer, the press had a field day with headlines such as "Elvis—Fat and Forty" appearing in the tabloids. It was reported that Elvis's live shows were growing sloppier and that maybe he should retire.

Sometimes he had taken so many drugs that he had to clutch the microphone stand just to stand up. He slurred words and forgot lyrics. His fans did not seem to care, and they packed the house whenever he appeared.

Elvis began to be hospitalized more often during his working engagements. He had a range of ailments: a weak heart, an enlarged colon, hypertension, and liver, kidney, and eye problems. He also continued to have problems with drug addiction, which did not help any of these chronic health conditions.

During one of his last performances, Elvis changed some of the lyrics to "Can't Help Falling in Love with You," singing "Wise men know when it's time to go." It was a chilling phrase that suggests Elvis knew his own end was near.

The Death of Elvis Presley

Elvis died on August 16, 1977. Then-girlfriend Ginger Alden found him facedown on the bathroom floor, unconscious. The official cause of death was complications arising from cardiac arrhythmia, or an irregular heartbeat.

Throngs of dedicated fans turned out at Elvis's funeral to mourn the death of the king of rock and roll.

Although it has never been clearly proven that Elvis died of either a drug overdose or polypharmacy (the workings of many different kinds of drugs in the body), these may have been contributing factors in his death. A blood sample drawn at the autopsy revealed toxic levels of quaalude, as well as high levels of codeine, Valium, and other sedatives and narcotics.

However, the autopsy also showed that Elvis suffered from heart disease, or a hardening of the arteries.

As fans grieved, Memphis florists sold every last flower they had and had to obtain more from Nashville. There were five tons in all. Thousands of bouquets appeared at Graceland, only to disappear after the funeral when fans snatched the flowers for precious mementos. After an attempt was made to steal Elvis's body from a mausoleum, his burial site was moved to the meditation garden at Graceland.

Elvis Lives

There is a week-long vigil held annually at Graceland to commemorate Elvis's death. There are fans who insist that Elvis faked his death and that he has been spotted at various places around the world. It would seem that Elvis's death had little impact on his legendary popularity: Elvis recordings, photos, movies, and merchandise continue to be big business. There are countless Elvis books, novels, plays, velvet paintings, posters, magazines, fan clubs, Web sites, and even churches. Many entertainers make their livings as Elvis impersonators.

Elvis's musical achievement is clear: He pioneered rock and roll and influenced a generation of performers. His music and his image are synonymous with 1950s rock and roll, and his influence is evident even today. Although Elvis's 1960s and 1970s material differed from the material that had made him famous, Elvis sang all of his songs with soul. He made even trite lyrics and uninspired musical arrangements special. The scope of his musical vision embraced R & B, gospel, blues, and country music; from singing sweet ballads to growling rock songs. He was a gifted singer with many different vocal styles. In life, he was rich in the charisma that led young girls to faint with ecstasy when he appeared onstage. In death, he remains unforgettable and legendary. He is Elvis Presley, the one and only king of rock and roll. Long live the King.

SELECTED DISCOGRAPHY

1956 *Elvis Presley*

1956 *Elvis*

1957 *Jailhouse Rock*

1960 *Elvis Is Back*

1960 *His Hand in Mine*

1963 *Girls! Girls! Girls!*

1964 *Roustabout*

1965 *Girl Happy*

1967 *How Great Thou Art*

1969 *From Elvis in Memphis*

1970 *Elvis Back in Memphis*

1972 *He Touched Me*

1975 *Promised Land*

1977 *Elvis in Concert*

1977 *Moody Blue*

SELECTED FILMOGRAPHY

1956 *Love Me Tender*

1957 *Jailhouse Rock*

1958 *King Creole*

1960 *G.I. Blues*

1961 *Blue Hawaii*

1962 *Girls! Girls! Girls!*

1964 *Roustabout*

1964 *Viva Las Vegas*

1965 *Harum Scarum*

1966 *Frankie and Johnny*

1967 *Clambake*

1967 *Double Trouble*

1968 *Stay Away, Joe*

1969 *Change of Habit*

1969 *The Trouble With Girls*

GLOSSARY

acknowledge To recognize or take notice.

ballad A song that is usually sentimental and of a slow tempo.

catalyst Something that brings together many elements.

charisma Magnetic charm or appeal.

commemorative In remembrance of someone.

crooner A person who sings ballads.

demo tape A demonstration tape made by singers and songwriters to promote their work to record companies.

documentary A nonfiction film.

hypertension A physical ailment, marked by very high blood pressure.

induction The act of making someone a part of a group.

insomnia Having great difficulty sleeping.

jamboree A program containing varied forms of entertainment.

marquee A large sign over the entrance of a building, usually a theater.

polypharmacy The presence of many drugs in the body.

race music Term used to describe rhythm and blues (R & B) before 1949.

segregation Separating people because they are of a different race, color, or creed.

trite Not original; boring.

TO FIND OUT MORE

Elvis Presley Enterprises, Inc.
P.O. Box 16508
3734 Elvis Presley Boulevard
Memphis, TN 38186-0508
(901) 332-3322
(800) 238-2000

Rock and Roll Hall of Fame Foundation
1290 Avenue of the Americas
New York, NY 10104

Rock and Roll Hall of Fame and Museum
One Key Plaza
Cleveland, OH 44114
(888) 764-ROCK (7625)
Web site: http://www.rockhall.com

Web Sites

Elvis.com—The Official Site
http://www.elvis.com

Elvis Presley E-zine
http://www.elvisnews.com

Elvis Presley Online
http://www.elvispresleyonline.com.

Sun Studio
http://www.sunstudio.com

FOR FURTHER READING

Daily, Robert. *Elvis Presley: The King of Rock 'n' Roll*. New York: Franklin Watts, Inc., 1996.

Doss, Erika. *Elvis Culture: Fans, Faith & Image*. Lawrence, KS: University Press of Kansas, 1999.

Hardinge, Melissa. *Elvis Presley*. Broomall, PA: Chelsea House Publishers, 1999.

Rubel, David. *Elvis Presley: The Rise of Rock and Roll*. Brookfield, CT: Millbrook Press, Inc., 1991.

Works Cited

Guralnick, Peter. *Careless Love: The Unmaking of Elvis Presley*. New York: Little, Brown and Company, 2000.

Guralnick, Peter. *Last Train to Memphis*. New York: Little, Brown and Company, 2000.

Miller, James. *Flowers in the Dustbin: The Rise of Rock & Roll 1947–1977*. New York: Simon and Schuster, 1999.

INDEX

109

CREDITS

About the Author

Magdalena Alagna is an editor and freelance writer living in New York City.

Photo Credits

Cover, pp. 4, 5, 7, 9, 11, 12, 17, 18, 22, 24, 31, 35, 43, 47, 50, 55, 56, 58, 60, 62, 64, 67, 70, 73, 75, 80, 83, 99 © Michael Ochs Archive; p. 28 © Colin Escott/Michael Ochs Archive; p. 41 © Roger Garwood and Trish Ainslie/Corbis; pp. 44–45 © Corbis; p. 72 © Bettmann/Corbis; p. 85 © Jeff Albertson/Corbis; pp. 80, 87, 96, © AP/Wide World Photos.

Layout and Design

Thomas Forget